DATE DUE

JAN 0 5

GAYLORD			PRINTED IN U.S.A.

For Sam Oakley — N. D.

For Alan and Annabel — N. L.

Text copyright © 2004 by Nicola Davies
Illustrations copyright © 2004 by Neal Layton

First U.S. edition 2004

Library of Congress Cataloging-in-Publication Data

Davies, Nicola.
Poop : a natural history of the unmentionable / Nicola Davies ; illustrated by Neal Layton. — 1st U.S. ed.
p. cm.
ISBN 0-7636-2437-3
1. Defecation — Juvenile literature. 2. Animal behavior — Juvenile literature. [1. Defecation. 2. Feces.
3. Animals — Habits and behavior.] I. Layton, Neal, ill. II. Title.
QP159.D38 2004
573.4'9 — dc22   2003069567

10 9 8 7 6 5 4 3 2

Printed in China

This book was typeset in AT Arta.
The illustrations were done in ink and digitally colored.

Candlewick Press
2067 Massachusetts Avenue
Cambridge, Massachusetts 02140

visit us at www.candlewick.com

THE COMMON GENET ON THE OPPOSITE PAGE IS sniffing a big pile of POOP. You can find out why if you turn to page 31.

Poop

A Natural History of the Unmentionable

Nicola Davies

illustrated by **Neal Layton**

CANDLEWICK PRESS
CAMBRIDGE, MASSACHUSETTS

Grownups are shy about it . . .

Horses ignore it . . .

Dogs like to sniff it . . .

And babies do it in their diapers . . .

7

Poop, big jobs, number two. Whatever you call it, feces (to give it one of its proper names) are everywhere. We humans may find it revolting and embarrassing, but the truth is that just about every animal poops. Or, to put it scientifically, all animals defecate. And the feces that they make come in all shapes and sizes.

A TOUR OF POOP

Feces can be so distinctive that it's possible to identify an animal species just from its poop! Every animal has its own special sort of poop, so this is just a small sample of a huge variety of different poop (some were just too big or runny to fit on the page).

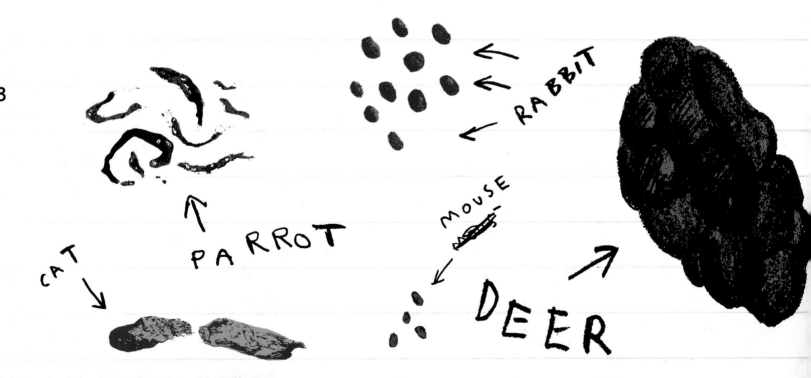

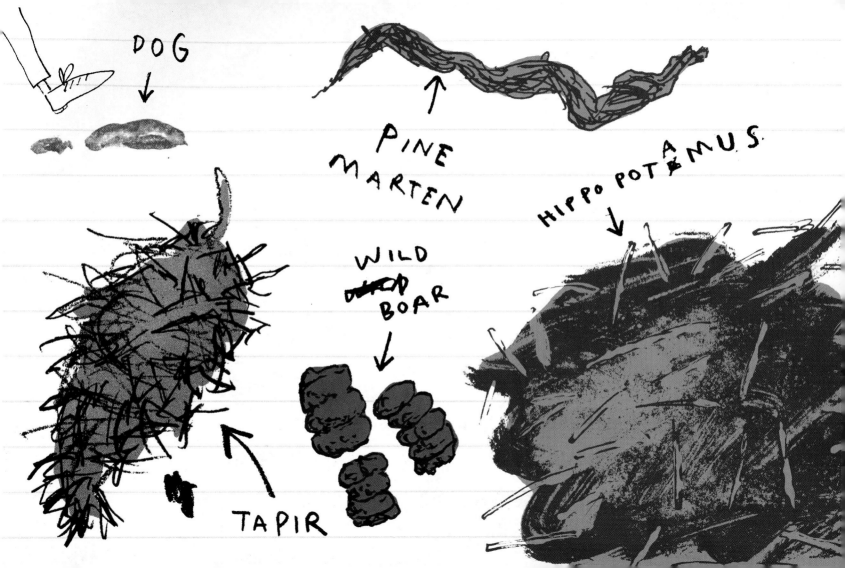

DOG

PINE MARTEN

HIPPOPOTAMUS

WILD ~~DOMESTIC~~ BOAR

TAPIR

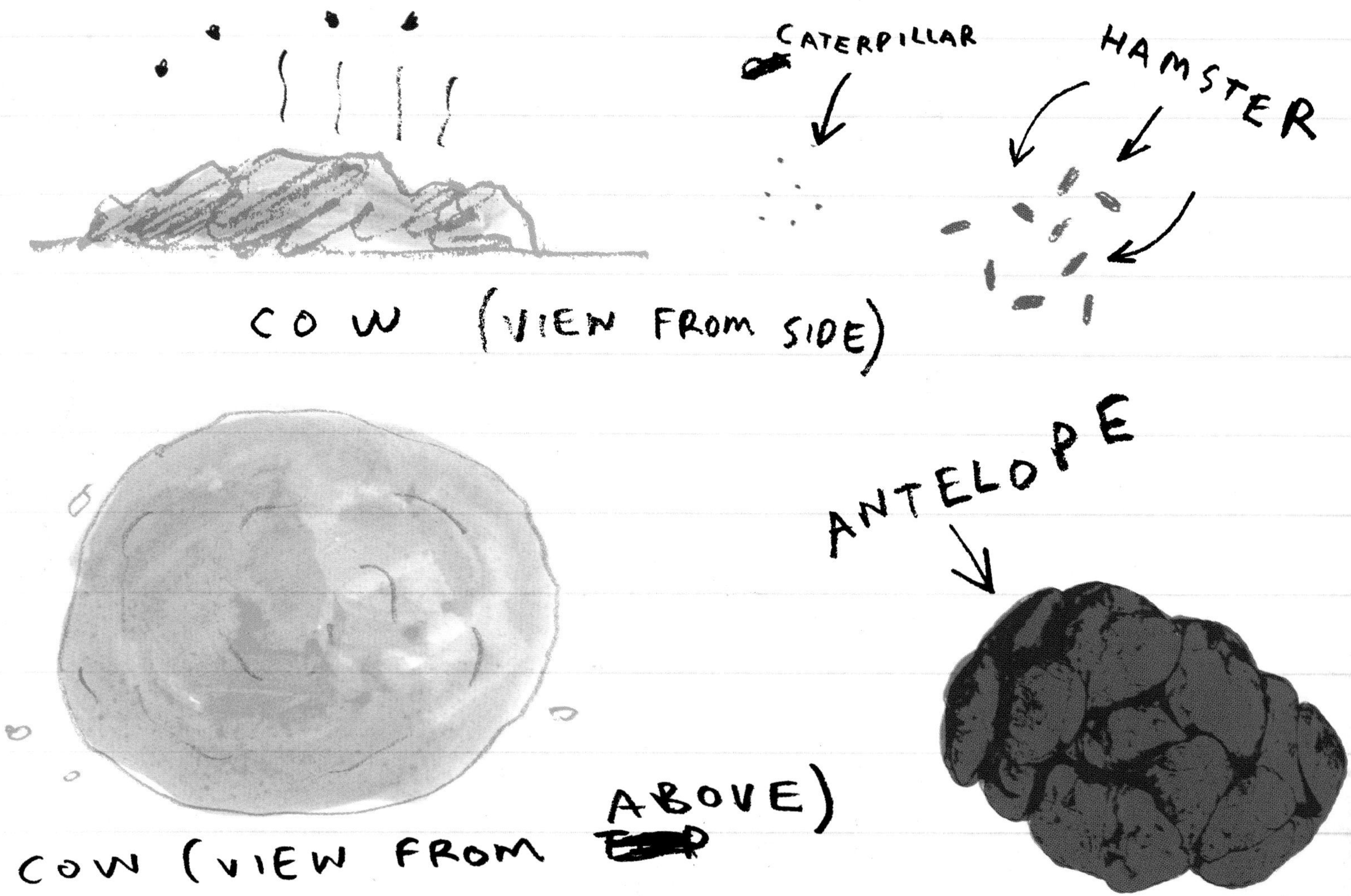

COW (VIEW FROM SIDE)

CATERPILLAR

HAMSTER

10

ANTELOPE

COW (VIEW FROM ~~ABOVE~~ ABOVE)

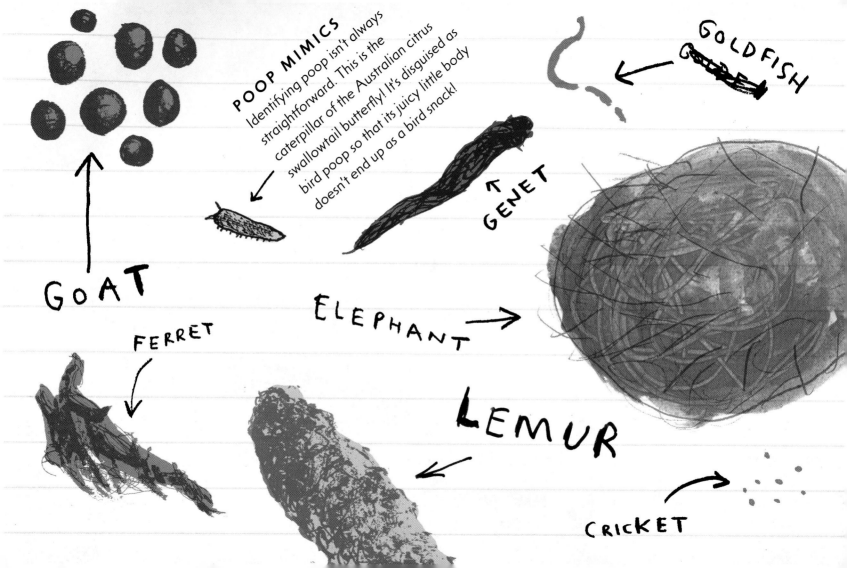

GOLDFISH

POOP MIMICS
Identifying poop isn't always straightforward. This is the caterpillar of the Australian citrus swallowtail butterfly! It's disguised as bird poop so that its juicy little body doesn't end up as a bird snack!

GENET

GOAT

FERRET

ELEPHANT

LEMUR

CRICKET

WHAT'S IT ALL FOR?

Sloppy or hard, skinny or fat, all this poop has a purpose: it's the way animals get rid of waste — not soda cans and candy wrappers, but body waste. What is body waste? Well, it's the remains of food that the body can't use, like worn-out blood cells, germs, and other unwanted material, such as worms that try to live inside the gut. As you can see, feces can contain quite a few different things.

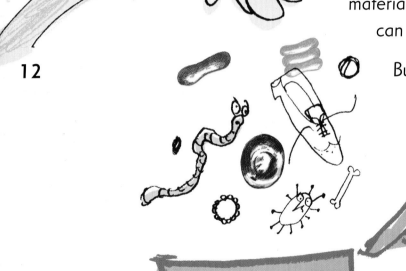

But mostly, poop is made of the pieces that are left after food has been chewed, swallowed, mixed, mashed, and digested from mouth to gut. And the reason that there are so many shapes and sizes of poop is that animals eat all kinds of different food.

Many animals also produce urine — wee, pee, tinkle, number one. Urine is another of the body's trash vehicles. It is made of waste discarded from the blood and then dissolved in water. It usually comes out through a different hole, but some animals, like birds, squirt urine and feces out together through the same opening. Insects don't really make urine at all and just produce feces that have their own special name, frass.

Meat-eating animals — such as tigers, lions, and foxes — have feces that usually look very different from those of plant eaters. Their poop contains hair, fur, feathers, and bone — in fact, any bits of the animals they have eaten. These bits tend to bind the poop together, making it long and untidy.

But the biggest difference between the poop of meat eaters (carnivores) and plant eaters (herbivores) is its quantity. Meat is a rich source of nourishment that's easy to digest, with very little waste. So carnivores don't need to eat or poop very often.

Plants are a lot less nourishing and difficult to digest, with lots of parts that are thrown away in feces. So herbivores need to eat almost all the time just to stay alive, and they hardly ever stop defecating.

15

Sheep are herbivores

SLOPPY OR PLOPPY?

JUST Like Grandma used to make.

VAMPIRE JAM

The other reason that poop comes in different shapes is its water content.

Vampire bats obviously feed on blood (not usually human), and blood is mostly water. So they get rid of the water by producing feces like runny jam. Camels are famous for their ability to go without water, and one way they manage it is by doing very dry poop.

16

But even animals that eat the same food have poop that can be very different. A cow produces about ten big sloppy pats, or cowpies, every day, but a sheep grazing on the same grass produces hundreds of little round droppings like currants. Why? The answer is that sheep hardly ever drink. They get water from the plants they eat, so by the time the grass has become poop, it's pretty dry and breaks into little pieces. But cows love to drink: they don't need to take moisture from the grass, so their poop can be like thick soup!

A VERY DRY CAMEL POOP

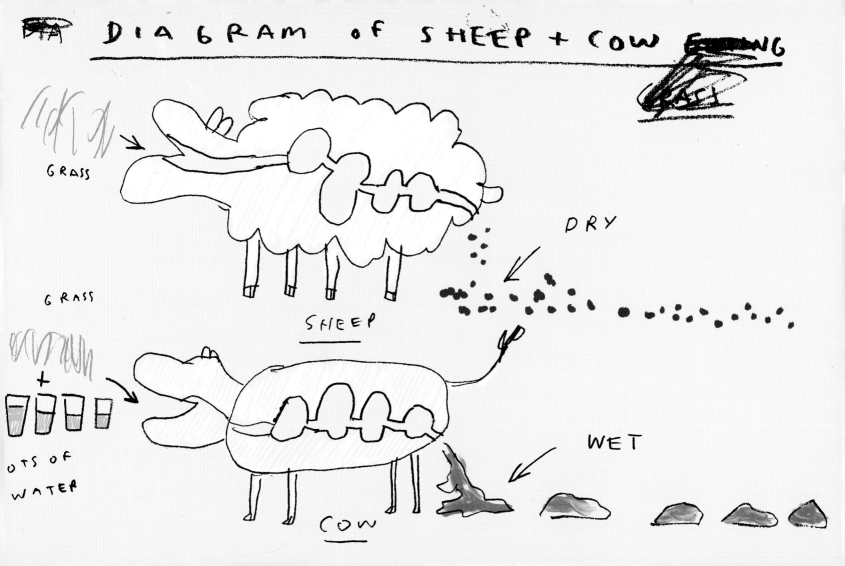

DIAGRAM of SHEEP + COW EATING

GRASS

GRASS

GRASS

SHEEP

DRY

COW

+

LOTS OF WATER

WET

RAINBOW POOP

The one thing that doesn't seem to vary much between different kinds of poop is color. Most is brownish or blackish. One reason for this is that mixing all the different colors in food is like mixing all the colors on a palette of paint — you get a kind of dark, yucky color. Another reason is that when a body digests food, it breaks down some of the colors it contained, leaving it dull and grayish. When this is added to the dark brown remains of dead blood cells, hey, presto — you get the familiar poop brown! Bird feces are usually a typical dark yucky color, too. But their droppings are splotched with white because their white and pasty urine leaves their body through the same hole as their poop.

Sometimes an animal may eat so much of a brightly colored food that the color gets through to the poop (as anyone who's eaten beets will know). Birds feasting on berries in the autumn can have droppings that look like peppermint candy — pink or mauve from the berries, and striped with white. Blue whales, too, can have tinted feces. When they feed on pink shrimp — swallowing a ton in a single mouthful — they do huge pink poop that looks like giant blobs of strawberry ice cream breaking up in the water.

← BLUE-WHALE POOP

PROBLEMS SOLVED WITH POOP

Poop may be mostly the leftovers from food, but some animals — herbivores in particular — have such a hard time getting nourishment from their food that reusing these leftovers can help.

Rabbits, for example, simply can't get all the nourishment they need from their food unless they digest it twice. And the simplest way to do that is to feast on their own feces. First, a bunny eats fresh green leaves or grass, which passes through its digestive system and pops out as soft, dark pellets of poop. The bunny eats these, still warm, straight from its bottom, and the food gets digested for a second time. After that, the bunny has gotten all the nourishment it can from its meal, so the next batch of fecal pellets is just waste and is deposited above ground.

Koalas have problems digesting their food too. They eat eucalyptus leaves, which are tough, full of poisons, and very hard to digest. The only way koalas can get what they need from their unappetizing diet is with the help of tiny microscopic creatures in their gut, called microbes, that do the job for them. But baby koalas aren't born with this band of tiny helpers, so the mother koala gives the baby some of hers — by feeding the youngster a little meal of poop, which is full of the gut microbes!

KOALA and BABY

CUTE BUNNY STORY

N.B. DON'T TRY THIS AT HOME...

Many other herbivores pass on these essential digestive helpers when their babies eat food with an accidental splash of their mother's feces on it. Baby elephants, however, sometimes want to be sure they've got their microbes, so they eat some of Mom's poop on purpose! Just one meal of this kind is enough to get the tiny helpers into the gut.

Poop eating — whether on purpose or by accident — is useful to a whole group of other sneaky creatures called parasites. Some parasites, such as tapeworms and roundworms, can live inside other animals' intestines, where they stay cozy and well fed. The worms also put their eggs into their hosts' feces. The eggs get eaten with the poop and hatch out inside their new home.

23

Meat-eating animals occasionally eat plant eaters' poop — just for the smell. Eating the feces of their prey helps predators to smell like the animals they need to catch, so they can sneak up on them without their own scent giving them away. Pet dogs still have this habit left over from the time when their ancestors had to hunt for dinner, instead of getting it in a bowl.

WHERE'S MY DINNER?

Predators look for useful clues about where to find dinner by checking out their prey's poop. Nice fresh poop can mean that food is close at hand. Baby animals make easy meals, so their feces are like a sign saying "Dinner is served." That's why some animal parents get rid of their youngsters' poop. Then, when the parents go out, predators won't know that young ones are alone.

24 Many small birds, for example, are incredibly picky about leaving droppings lying around the nest. After they've been fed, the baby birds obediently turn around, stick their bums up over the edge of the nest, and produce a nice neat dropping with a coating on the outside that acts like a bag. The mom or dad bird picks up the poop, flies off with it, and then drops it somewhere out of sight.

Most small animals have to watch out for predators even when they're fully grown. Golden moles from southern Africa stay underground all the time because they are just about snack-size as far as a bird of prey or a jackal is concerned. But the moles don't want to have feces all over their homes, so they keep one little chamber in their large burrows just for pooping in.

← DIAGRAM SHOWING THE INSIDE OF A GOLDEN MOLE BURROW

TOILET TALK

Golden moles aren't alone in having a special place to poop. Latrines, as these animal toilets are known, are quite common in nature and are used for a lot more than just pooping.

Giant otters, which live in big family groups in the rivers of South America, have giant latrines, and making and using them is a family affair. All the otters in the group trample an area of the riverbank bigger than a pool table. When the area is flat, the otters poop all over it. The smell is overpowering, and the flattened plants on the bank can be seen from far up and down the river. The latrine isn't just a toilet — it's a great big message for any new otter in town: "This is our river, and there are so many of us that we've done all this poop. So you better get lost."

OOOPS... WRONG TURN...

In fact, sending messages is what latrines are all about. Badgers, which also live in family groups, use latrines to mark the edges of their territory. They dig small pits and poop in them, leaving a smelly signal saying, "This is our patch. Keep out!" Tigers and other big cats leave their feces in special piles of earth, called scrapes, to say the same thing. Male hippos like to spread their message around. They quickly waggle their tails as they defecate, spraying their poop — and its macho message about how big and tough they are — in all directions.

Latrines and poop in general can be used to send more complicated messages, too. Poop can contain all sorts of different smells. A quick sniff can tell an animal who did the poop, how old they were, what sex they were, and if they were head of the gang or bottom of the pile! What's more, the strength of the smell fades with time, so it's possible to tell when the poop was done — today, yesterday, or last week. All this can make a latrine into a kind of bulletin board.

Peccaries, wild pigs from the South American jungle, live in big gangs. When everyone is busy finding food all day, it can be hard to keep up with one another's social lives. Peccaries have a big latrine in the center of their territory that everybody uses. And each time a peccary poops, it has a good old sniff of the latrine to find out what's going on in the group — who's around, who's pregnant, who's ready to mate, who's boss, and who wants to be!

Rabbits are group-living animals that use latrines like bulletin boards, too. Any slight mound can become a latrine where lots of different rabbits come to defecate. With tens or even hundreds of rabbits living in a maze of burrows, a good sniff of a latrine keeps a rabbit up-to-date with what's going on.

Latrines can also be important for solitary animals, which sometimes use them as a "lonely hearts" advertisement to find a mate. Genets, small spotted catlike animals from Africa and southern Europe, hunt and live alone. They have latrines in prominent places, such as the top of a big tree, a building's high flat roof, or a big rock. Any genet passing through the area is bound to find a latrine, and in one sniff it knows if any possible mates or likely rivals are in the area.

Sloths have perhaps the most extreme toilet-using habits of any animal. They live solitary lives, high in the treetops of South American rain forests, where they eat leaves, leaves, and more leaves. Unlike many other herbivores, they don't defecate very often. Every four days a sloth climbs down from its treetop home to poop in its own private latrine at the base of a tree. The piles of dung at these latrines can be huge and very smelly, and since sloths don't see much of one another, checking out the poop at the latrines is almost the only way they keep in touch.

NAVIGATION BY NOSE (AND BOTTOM)

The lasting smell of feces makes them useful to animals in many different ways. Hippos also use their poop for navigation, for example. At night they leave the rivers to eat grass on dry land, marking their trail with piles of dung. Even on the darkest nights, the hippos can find their way back by following the smell of their poop.

33

WHAT'S HAPPENING TO ALL THAT POOP?

A single hippo can add several pounds of poop to a signpost dung pile in one night, and yet the piles never get any bigger. And of course hippos aren't the only ones producing large amounts of feces. All over the world, animals are defecating all of the time. Imagine all those billions of tons of poop!

What happens to it all? All sorts of things!

A small amount of poop gets reused for building. Millipedes make a nest for their eggs from their own poop, using the tiny pellets of feces like miniature bricks. In Africa, ovenbirds, which make complicated predator-proof mud nests, use the dung of large animals like antelope, water buffalo, and domestic cattle, especially when water is short and mud is hard to find.

Some termites use their poop to make gardens! Termites eat wood, which is so hard to digest that some species don't bother. They just chew it up and poop it out. Then they stick their poop together to make lumps, called combs, and grow mushrooms on them. These mushroom gardens deep in the termite mound provide food for the whole colony.

Even humans have used poop as a cheap building material. Hundreds of years ago, most ordinary houses were built from a mixture of mud and cow dung slapped onto a frame of woven willow branches. In some countries, cattle dung is still used to help build houses and is burned as fuel where wood is scarce.

PROFESSIONAL POOP EATERS

The real reason that we're not up to our necks in feces is that one animal's poop is another animal's lunch. There are plenty of animals that make a living by feeding on feces that aren't theirs, a habit that has the scientific name coprophagy. Some of the most extraordinary of these poop eaters, or coprophages, are dung beetles. Seeing them at work, you can see how so much poop disappears so quickly. In Africa, within minutes of elephant poop hitting the ground in a great steaming pile, there is a whir of wings as the dung beetles arrive and set to work.

Some dive straight into the dung, and others tunnel beneath it and bury it. Some roll balls of the dung away and bury them deep underground. But all of them eat it and lay eggs on it, and when those eggs hatch, the dung provides food for the beetle grubs. Within two hours, up to 16,000 dung beetles might have arrived and made the elephant feces disappear!

There are 7,000 different types of dung beetle all over the world, and they each have a favorite kind of poop. Some small species like the ready-rolled balls of rabbit feces. Others prefer a big pile of cow or horse dung. Desert dung beetles collect poop as dry and hard as concrete and bury it deep in moist sand so that it gets soft enough to eat. Rain forest dung beetles can climb around in tree branches eighty feet high. They scrape monkey poop off the leaves, then bring it down to the forest floor to bury it.

39

These beetles are tree planters, because monkeys eat fruit whose seeds come out in monkey feces and then get buried along with their poop.

Australian farmers discovered how important dung beetles were when they introduced cows to Australia. Australian dung beetles were used to the dainty and delicate little poop of kangaroos and wallabies — they'd never seen cow dung before and couldn't manage those big pats. So the cow poop just sat in the sun, covering more and more land and giving millions and millions of flies a perfect place to breed. In some places there were so many flies that they filled the air and it was hard to breathe. Then in 1967 biologists brought dung beetles that were used to big-scale poop from other countries and released them in Australia. The dung beetles loved it, and soon the cow pats and the flies were disappearing from the Australian countryside. The people of Cootaburra, a small town in South Australia, were so grateful to the beetles that they made a model of a dung beetle six stories high on a hill outside the town so no one would ever forget how important dung beetles are.

In other parts of the world, including Europe and North America, there have always been large animals with big poop. So the feces of horses and cows get cleared away by native dung beetles and more than one hundred other species of insects. What the insects can't finish, worms, fungi, and microbes can. Poop doesn't stand a chance and is used up in only a few weeks.

HOLY BAT POOP

GEE WHIZ, LOOK AT ALL THAT POOP!

MOM!

Not all feces disappear so quickly, because sometimes there's just so much of it that the cleanup takes years. Fifty tons of poop falls on the floor of Bracken Cave in Texas every day from the bottoms of the 20 million bats that live there. Across the world there are many similar caves that are home to millions of bats, with floors many feet deep in bat droppings. In some of them, bat researchers even ski on the mountains of poop.

With such a huge food supply, it isn't surprising that there are many tiny mouths busily eating it. In one bat cave in Trinidad, researchers counted a million poop eaters in a single patch of feces the size of a picnic table. There were mites the size of pinheads and cockroaches as long as your little finger. All these coprophages make meals for other creatures: toads eat the cockroaches, and snakes and opossums eat the toads! No matter how much bat poop the coprophages eat, they never run out because every dawn a new supply is delivered fresh by air! This fabulous food supply makes bat caves such a good home that some animals never leave: Niah Cave in Borneo has a kind of poop-eating earwig and a species of earwig-eating gecko that are found nowhere else on Earth!

43

THE ONE and ONLY...

AND I EAT EARWIGS!

I EAT POOP!

FECAL FARMERS

Some kinds of ants go one step further than just eating feces: they actually farm other animals for their poop. Greenflies feed by sticking their needlelike mouth-parts into a plant and letting its nice, sugary sap flow into their bodies. It's a diet that's very high in water, so as they eat, the greenflies are always defecating, and their poop is very like their food — a sugary liquid. Ants walk among the greenflies, stroking them with their legs to squeeze out the sappy poop, which the ants eat straight from the greenflies' bottoms.

44   We humans think that we invented recycling with our collections of old newspapers and special bins for cans and bottles, but nature has been recycling for billions of years — since life on Earth first began. Poop and the living things that feed on it are a big part of that natural recycling, helping to break down the remains of plant and animal bodies into smaller and smaller pieces that can return to the soil for plants to reuse.
This recycling happens very quietly and almost invisibly, but its effect is huge. Without it, life on Earth would stop very quickly.

APHID

SPECIAL DELIVERY

So plants need poop to refill their food supplies in the soil. But that's not the only job poop does for plants: it can be their mail carrier too! Many animals eat fruits and berries and the plant seeds inside them. The seeds are carried from the parent plant in the animals' stomachs and pop out later in feces, delivered to a new place where they can sprout and grow — which is exactly what the plant wants. In fact, many plants make berries or fruits that will attract a particular kind of animal *because* its poop makes the best mail carrier!

In the tropics, many trees and bushes have juicy green fruits that hang clear of their leaves. These are perfect for attracting bats, which have big appetites, need a clear flight path, and because they feed at night, don't find fruits by their color.

After they've feasted on fruit, bats don't stop to poop but often do it while flying over clearings in the forest. This makes them perfect seed deliverers, as they take seeds to areas where there are no plants to compete with. Thanks to bat poop, areas that are completely bare of plants can be covered in thriving young shrubs and trees in just a couple of years.

THAT'S MY JOB!!

In northern climates, many plants have seeds that are spread by birds. Birds find food by sight, and outside the tropics, fruit-eating birds tend to be small. So the small bright berries of many woodland and hedgerow plants, such as hawthorn, holly, and honeysuckle, are perfect to tempt birds to eat them and carry away the seeds. The berries are green until the seeds inside are ripe and ready to start a new life. Then the berries turn red and sweet, a signal to the birds that dinner is served.

Mistletoe is the cleverest plant of all at getting birds — and their poop — to work for it. The white mistletoe berries that we use to decorate our homes at Christmas are a favorite food of many birds, like thrushes, blackbirds, and robins. They eat the berries, but the seeds of the mistletoe that come out in their droppings are very sticky and cling uncomfortably to the birds' bottoms. The only way a bird can get rid of them is to wipe its bottom vigorously on a rough piece of bark or a crack in a branch. This is exactly what the plant needs. The bird has, without knowing it, planted the seeds in the place where they are most likely to survive: a crevice on a tree branch where the mistletoe plant can easily take root.

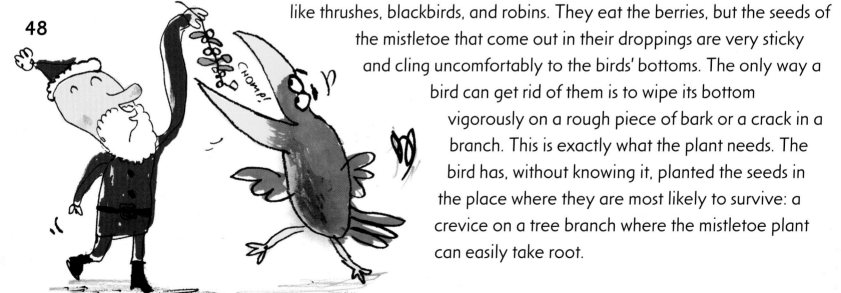

POOP DETECTIVES

Seeds are made extra strong to survive chewing and digestion, and there are other hard parts of food, such as bones and shells, that pop out again as good as new. These leftovers can be useful if you want to know what an animal eats, especially if you can't watch it feeding.

Sperm whales hunt in the deepest water, up to 8,000 feet below the surface, where it is always cold and dark. At this depth the water pressure would crush a human like an ant, so no one can follow a sperm whale to see what it eats. But just before a sperm whale dives from the surface to these mysterious depths, it defecates, and if a whale scientist is quick, the poop can be scooped up in a net. The hard parts in the sperm whale's poop are horny jaws and teeth belonging to squid and sharks. By looking at them carefully, scientists now know that sperm whales can eat big sharks, and squid up to sixty-five feet long.

Bats, too, are almost impossible to watch when they are out catching insects to eat. Luckily, insects like moths, flies, and beetles have a hard outside shell made of stuff called chitin. So, tiny chewed-up fragments of the insect's chitin shell come out in bat feces. You can see them under a microscope — fragments of wing, shreds of leg, scraps of head. With a little patience, these parts can be matched with whole insects to show which ones the bat has been eating. It is even possible to tell how many insects a bat ate by counting the numbers of insect legs or eyes. Bat researchers all over the world have used this method to discover what bats have been up to. One study showed that a colony of just 150 big brown bats in Arizona ate enough beetles in one summer to protect local farmers from 18 million pest insects!

8764, 8765, 8766, 8767...

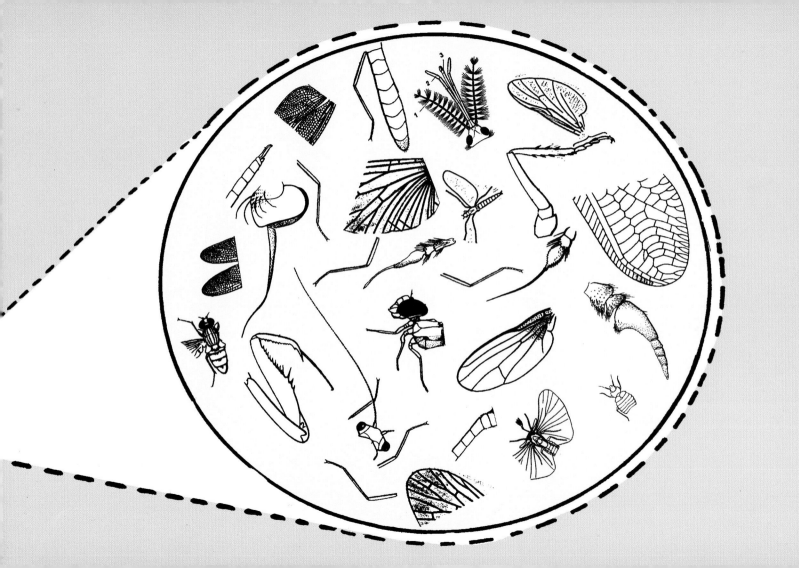

FOSSIL POOP

Of course, the hardest animals of all to study are extinct ones. No one will ever see a Tyrannosaurus rex eating its dinner, but along with fossils of its skeleton, T. rex has left some fossil poop, called coprolites. Coprolites found with T. rex bones in Canada contained fragments of a triceratops's ribs.

What's more, the ribs had tooth marks that matched T. rex teeth, showing that the big predators had slashed their teeth along the side of a triceratops, ripping flesh and bones. T. rex poop had shown not only what was for dinner 70 million years ago but also how it was eaten!

MORE THINGS TO DO WITH POOP

Feces can be a great tool in the detective work involved in finding out about the lives of some of the most elusive animals. Otters are so shy that it's very hard to watch them in the wild, but they leave their droppings, or spraints, wherever they go. Each spraint contains enough of an otter's unique genetic code — its DNA — to tell exactly which otter left it and how that otter is related to other otters in the area. So by collecting spraints and studying their DNA, researchers can tell exactly who pooped where and when. This information tells the researchers how otters use their habitat and who is related to whom.

56 A much simpler method of working out who goes where can be used with wild animals that will take food put out for them by humans. Badgers and foxes are exceptionally greedy and will finish off all kinds of scraps. If the food contains a harmless dye, then all you have to do to find out where the animal travels over the next two days is find all the brightly colored feces. Good thing badgers and foxes are almost colorblind, or they might worry about doing technicolor poop!

There are as many good stories about poop as there are kinds of animals. The ones in this book are just a small selection. As we've seen, poop can be used for food, fuel, and building material. It delivers messages, spreads seeds, and recycles nutrients to keep life on Earth going. Poop is probably the most useful stuff on the planet. It's no surprise that a bird poop on your head is supposed to be lucky!

POOP FACTS

Biggest: Blue whale. The biggest animals in the world make the biggest poop: ten inches wide and several yards long.

Smallest: Bumblebee bat. This tiny bat weighs less than a tenth of an ounce and does droppings the size of a pinhead.

COMPACT AND BIJOU!

Highest: Maned wolf. It has long legs and always defecates standing up, so it can leave its poop on objects three feet off the ground.

Smelliest: Orangutans poop after they have been eating durian fruit. Durian fruit smells pretty bad to start with, so after it's been inside an orangutan and out again . . .

Weirdest: Mayflies, simply because they don't poop at all. They live for only one day. Since they don't eat, they don't need to poop!

INDEX

Woof

GLOSSARY

carnivore a meat eater
coprolite fossilized poop
coprophage a poop eater
   (someone else's poop, at that)
defecation pooping
dung poop
feces poop
fecal pellets poop
forbivore a grass eater
frass insect poop
graminivore a grain eater
herbivore a plant eater
latrine toilet
microbes microscopic creatures
number one pee
number two poop
omnivore an animal that eats both
   meat and plants
parasite an animal or plant that lives
   in or on another animal or plant
pat sloppy poop
piscivore a fish eater
spraints poop
urine pee
vegetarian a human herbivore

YUM!

GRR!

61